Advanced Praise for

MOTIVATED
BY THE
WORD

Use *Motivated By The Word* for contemplation, introspection, and as a guide for your daily meditation and devotion. This book will help you understand what's around you, and what's going on inside you. Plan a course of action as you endeavor to elevate your spiritual growth and understanding.

I use this book to check myself, reset myself, and encourage myself.

~Berena Hughes

Motivated By The Word is a valuable resource that can be tackled at your own pace—weekly, monthly or however you flow with it.

Kenya Z. Edwards requires us to look deeper into the "whys" and "whats" of our actions. These twenty four words dare us to look beyond the surface.

~Tojuan Minus, Author
Girl, I See You: Conversations Women Need to Have

MOTIVATED
BY THE
WORD

MOTIVATED BY THE WORD

24 MEDITATIONS TO CAPTURE YOUR INNER STRENGTHS

KENYA Z. EDWARDS

DEDICATION

To my mother, **Carol Howard** for creating the woman that I am today.

FOREWORD

Kenya and I met while matriculating at SUNY Brockport and we became fast friends. Even then, her passion for life and zeal for knowledge was evident. After school and as life moved us in different directions, we stayed in touch (sometimes infrequently). Through life's vicissitudes and challenges, I've witnessed the hand of the LORD on her. She has weathered storms, which have made her stronger and wiser for God's assignments in His Kingdom. She is an unapologetic disciple of the Lord Jesus Christ and is a compassionate soul which is manifested in her relatability to so many people.

Motivated By The Word is an inspiring, impactful, and insightful book on how to meditate on God, through His Word, and to practically apply His principals in everyday life. This book can be life changing for the unbeliever of Jesus Christ, as well as the believer in Jesus Christ. Kenya Z. Edwards has given her readers a powerful tool to help transform their spirits, souls, and minds.

Pastor Wilbur Phillips, Jr.
First Baptist Church, Delair, NJ

ACKNOWLEDGEMENTS

I would like to extend my heartfelt thanks to the many people who made this book possible.

A special thank you to my family, for your endless patience and love. To my son, **Matthew** for standing by my side in all things of God, through all things of God, and for all things of God. **Chrystal R. Howard, and Carleen Burke-Fernandes**, your belief in me gave me the courage to follow this path. I love you all.

Berena Hughes, for being my proofreader - reviser – checker. Your sharp eyes can spot a double space from a mile away. Thank you for ensuring that my voice was accurately perceived. It was your thoughtful guidance that helped me shape this into what it is today. Your insight was invaluable throughout this process.

To my Scribe Coach, **Penda L. James**, for believing in this project from the beginning and always championing my work.

To my friends and fellow writers, **Latifa Miller, Angila Curvey-Chukwu, and Becky Arnold Antkowiak,** your encouragement and feedback have been a source of strength and inspiration. I couldn't have made it through the late nights and rewrites without your support.

To the **readers and listeners of "What Would Kay Say?"** your engagement and support inspire me every day. I'm so grateful to be able to share this journey with you. Thank you all for being a part of this chapter in my life.

To **everyone else** - too many to mention by name, thank you for your support and for keeping the faith.

The twenty-four elders fall down before Him who sits on the throne and worship Him who lives forever and ever, and cast their crowns before the throne, saying:

"You are worthy, O Lord, To receive glory and honor and power;
For You created all things, And by Your will they exist and were created."

Revelation 4:10-11 (NKJV)

HOW TO USE THIS BOOK

Words carry power—more power than we often attribute to them. A word spoken in a specific situation can undoubtedly bring about change, especially when it is spoken and received as God intends. With this understanding, God inspired me to write *Motivated By The Word: 24 Meditations To Capture Your Inner Strengths*. I was curious about the significance of the number 24. Why would God want me to write a book centered around this concept and this specific number?

Upon researching, I discovered that biblically, the number 24 represents the complete Church. It is the sum of the 12 tribes of Israel and the 12 Apostles of the Lamb of God. Additionally, the number 24 is associated with the priesthood, who oversee God's work on Earth. Interestingly, the number 24 also represents the number of books in the Hebrew Bible or Tanakh (Wikipedia).

In the Book of Revelation, there were 24 elders seated on 24 thrones. Revelation 4:4 (NKJV) states: "Around the throne were twenty-four thrones, and on the thrones I saw twenty-four elders sitting, clothed in white robes; and they had crowns of gold on their heads." The story continues, revealing the significance of the number 24 and why we must also consider it an important part of our lives. Revelation 4:10-11 (NKJV) further elaborates: " the twenty-four elders fall down before Him who sits on the throne and worship Him who lives forever and ever, and cast their crowns before the throne, saying: You are worthy, O Lord, To receive glory and honor and power; For You created all things, And by Your will they exist and were created."

The relationship of the number 24 extends further. The number 2 symbolizes balance, relationship, cooperation, and partnership. It reflects our great commission and purpose, as seen when Jesus sent the disciples out in pairs (Luke 10:1). Meanwhile, the number 4 signifies physical and spiritual completeness. In Genesis 1:4, God separated light from darkness, creating a complete day. The number 4 also represents the promises God made to Abraham when He formed the Covenant: land, posterity, blessings, and salvation. Jesus the Messiah is a descendant of Abraham, to whom God promised that He would be his God.

In this book *Motivated By The Word*, there is a recurring theme of balance, home, health, integrity, relationship, and wisdom. God seeks to mold the character within you for His glory. He wants to bring out and work through all the wonderful characteristics He has placed in you. As you read through this book, meditate on each word. This devotional is intended to accompany your daily study of God's word or your personal growth.

You decide how to use this book to your advantage. You can meditate on one word monthly, allowing it to bring about the changes the Lord wants in your life. You can focus on a word daily or weekly if you are seeking rapid movement of God in your life. In either case, God is seeking to empower your spirit with consistency.

A mature Christian looks forward to running the best race. *Motivated By The Word* was written to help you tap into what God is saying. Think about what He is telling you about your family, your relationships, and how you govern your life. Before you move forward in this book, ask God for His guidance as you begin this journey. If you don't have a personal relationship with a higher power, perhaps this book can lead you to establishing one, allowing you the opportunity to connect with the Creator of all living things. I pray this book brings you the same joy in reading it as it did for me in writing it.

CONTENTS

1

CAPTURING YOUR INNER STRENGTHS
RESILIENT

*(adj.) able to withstand or recover quickly
from difficult conditions*

In the journey of life, challenges and obstacles are
inevitable. Yet, it is not merely about enduring
these trials but about embracing them with
resilience and strength, anchored in faith. Just as
athletes train rigorously to build physical stamina,
we too must equip ourselves mentally, physically,
and spiritually to navigate the complexities of life.
With each trial we face, our endurance is tested,
and our faith is strengthened. As we continue to
run the race set before us, may we never lose sight
of the source of our strength. Through
unwavering faith and reliance on the Holy Spirit,
we can overcome any obstacle and emerge
victorious.

As I reflect upon those words, I am reminded of a time in my life when I faced my greatest challenge: the passing of my mom. In the Bible, God stresses the concept of family, but reading it and living it out are two very different scenarios. My mom had great Biblical insight when it came to investing, following the outline of God's interpretation when it came to the structure of family. She was able to acquire multiple properties, but unfortunately, did not leave a will.

It was understood in the family that I would receive the two-family home that I occupied with her upon her death—or so I thought. By agreeing to care for my mom (being the baby of the family), I put aside my aspirations of homeownership, all the while witnessing my mom assist my siblings in attaining their versions of the American Dream. You can imagine my surprise when I was confronted with court dates to "settle" the estate. My siblings (there were six of us, but now only three of us remain) all possessed their own property; what could we possibly have to settle? But know this: in the midst of the situation, you will develop a resilient spirit. I did. One that allowed me to hold fast to the promises that God was more than able to keep me. He was also more than able to sustain me through every trial until the day of victory. It is in times of extreme difficulty that I find solace in prayer. I am able to draw daily upon the strength given to me through Jesus Christ. With faith as my guide, I press on, knowing I am empowered to triumph over every challenge that comes my way. The race is not given to the swift but to the one who endures until the end.

For this reason I also suffer these things; nevertheless I am not ashamed, for I know whom I have believed and am persuaded that He is able to keep what I have committed to Him until that Day.

2 Timothy 1:12 (NKJV)

REFLECT ON THE WORD

How have you developed your ability to remain resilient during challenging times in your life?

Have you ever felt the need to sacrifice your personal goals or aspirations for family obligations?

How did that experience shape your outlook on family and responsibility?

In what ways can faith, spirituality, or a sense of purpose serve as a foundation for developing resilience? How do you stay grounded in your beliefs during times of uncertainty?

PRAYER

God,

I ask that You give us the strength to continue this race by drawing on the Holy Spirit daily. Let us look to our Comforter for the assistance needed to develop the resilient spirits required to handle unforeseen circumstances. Lord, with that spirit, we will be able to withstand any form of opposition that the enemy brings to our path.

In Jesus' name.

Amen.

2

VISION FOR PURPOSEFUL LIVING
INTENTIONAL

(adj.) done on purpose; deliberate.

To live a life of intention signifies a deep commitment to carrying out God's will every day. It involves aligning your actions with your divine purpose and embracing opportunities to impact others positively. Whether it's showing kindness to the elderly, teaching in Sunday school, or aiding the less fortunate, each endeavor becomes part of God's overarching plan. Much like the servants in the parable of the talents, faithful execution of God's given tasks leads to growth and multiplication.

I remember when I first felt the nudging of my spirit to begin exploring my purpose. It seemed like I attended every conference on Public Speaking and Speech Writing. It was overwhelming, to say the least, and I was a bit apprehensive due to the uncertainty of it all. How was I going to know what to say, whom to say it to, or when to say it? How could I be the voice that God wanted to use to get His message into the world? These are the questions I pondered over and over in my head.

One day, the Holy Spirit reminded me that the vision I was carrying was about more than just me. I needed to take myself out of the equation, trust the calling placed on my life, and understand that it included numerous individuals whose lives were hanging in the balance. These individuals were waiting for me to actively engage in the purpose that I was given. After all, how could they do their part in God's tapestry if I didn't intentionally do mine?

All of this reinforces in my mind that for God to believe we are ready for the task set before us, we have to pursue our gifts and talents with vigor and enthusiasm. We have to be intentional in our cooperation with God's agenda for our lives, which ultimately means becoming the shining lights that will glorify God and positively influence the world around us.

As I walk this journey, it is my heart's desire to live an intentional life, seeking His wisdom to complete the task in conjunction with expressions of gratitude for His grace and mercy.

Then the Lord answered me and said: Write the vision and make it plain on tablets, That he may run who reads it.

Habakkuk 2:1 (NKJV)

REFLECT ON THE WORD

Have you decided to live an intentional life for the Kingdom?

If so, how has this changed your perspective of your Christian walk?

If not, what is holding you back?

PRAYER

Lord,

I seek Your guidance to live my life with your vision in mind. As your child I stay, in Your presence grateful for Your grace and mercy. My life is devoted to You. I dedicate myself to fulfilling the purposes that You have entrusted to me. Every second, every minute, and every hour, You have my unwavering faith and assurance that I am committed and will remain intentional in all I do.

In Jesus' name,

Amen.

3

GUIDANCE WITH OBEDIENCE
DISCIPLINE

(n) the practice of training people to obey rules or a code of behavior, using punishment to correct disobedience

Chastisement is often viewed as a form of discipline and is akin to a caring parent warning a child about the dangers of touching a hot stove. Similarly, our Heavenly Father corrects us out of love, guiding us away from harm and towards the path of righteousness. As an omniscient being, God comprehends the perils we encounter when we disobey and succumb to sin.

The job posting stated: "The Construction Department is seeking a Second Level Manager to take on the responsibilities of the newly formed line/splicing department." This was the perfect position for me to advance up the corporate ladder. It was a promotion that not only offered a higher pay grade but would have established me as a leader in the industry. I possessed all the necessary credentials and experience needed for the position. We often feel that we know what is best for us and where we want our careers to go. However, when God has a plan for our life, it might not unfold exactly as we envision.

By allowing me to obtain that promotion, I would have postponed pursuing the direction God had given me a year earlier. Although I had told Him yes, this position would have fulfilled my own desires. As it turned out, the person who took the promotion became very ill due to the overwhelming demands of the job. It's essential to acknowledge that God operates with decency and order in all things. By accepting His correction, we demonstrate our readiness to follow His guidance. In doing so, we acknowledge that He possesses the ultimate capability to orchestrate everything for our benefit.

For whom the LORD loves He chastens, And scourges every son whom He receives.

Hebrews 12:6 (NKJV)

REFLECT ON THE WORD

Disappointment is never easy to accept. What has God withheld from you to protect you?

How has God shown you that He knows what is best for your life?

This chapter talks about God's correction being a form of love. Can you recall a time when a difficult situation or "chastisement" led to growth or clarity in your life?

PRAYER

Lord,

I wholeheartedly desire to walk in alignment with Your will. I welcome Your correction, understanding that it comes from a place of love and care for me. Lord, lead me into all truth so that my life may shine as a reflection of Your glory and bring honor to Your name. Illuminate my path with Your wisdom, guiding me in every decision and action I take. May my life be a testimony to Your goodness and grace, drawing others closer to You.

In Jesus' name,

Amen

When our actions stem from sincerity, they hold genuine value as offerings to God.

MOTIVATED
BY THE
WORD

4

HONORING GOD THROUGH CONSISTENCY
DILIGENT

(adj) - constant in effort to accomplish something; attentive and persistent in doing anything

The Bible tells us that the steps of a good man are ordered by the Lord, and if we delight ourselves in Him, He will grant us the desires of our hearts. As we follow those steps carefully laid before us, we are reminded to approach every endeavor as if serving the Lord directly. Our inner spirit urges us to seek perfection, avoiding shortcuts and incomplete efforts. This mindset embodies the earnest care and conscientiousness we invest in our tasks, recognizing them as offerings to the One deserving of all honor and praise. When our actions stem from sincerity, they hold genuine value as offerings to God. While our works alone do not secure our place in heaven—only the grace and mercy of Jesus accomplishes that—our diligence allows us to run the race faithfully until His return.

When given the directive to write a book, I was both excited and overwhelmed. A prophet had spoken over my life, stating that one day I would write a book. I assumed it would be just as he said; I would be writing a book about the women of God. I never thought of myself as a writer, although I had tried to write a screenplay in college and joked about writing my autobiography. Was this the gateway to writing my memoirs?

Putting questions aside, I began to write, and two years later, I accomplished this book. Diligence grounded in sincerity and dedicated to the Lord becomes a pathway to success. Striving for excellence infuses our efforts with deeper significance. Proverbs 12 emphasizes the importance of diligence, indicating that the diligent will ultimately prevail, while the idle wither away.

The hand of the diligent will rule,
But the negligent and lazy will be
put to forced labor.

Proverbs 12:24 (NKJV)

REFLECT ON THE WORD

What has God given you to do that requires your full attention in order to complete?

How has it changed the way you approach your Godly gifts and talents?

How can you approach being diligent in your life?

PRAYER

We seek you Lord for Your guidance, asking that the work of our hands be a sincere offering, bringing You praise and glory. May each task we accomplish align with Your purpose for our lives, ensuring that our efforts are not in vain.

In Jesus' name,

Amen.

Dominion, therefore, is not a passive privilege but an active responsibility.

MOTIVATED
BY THE
WORD

5

GOD'S DIVINE MISSION
DOMINION

(n) sovereignty or control

In the Book of Genesis, God bestows upon humanity the profound mandate of dominion over the earth, declaring that humans are created in His own image. However, Adam and Eve's disobedience led to the infiltration of sin into the world, thwarting God's intended plan for humanity to reflect His glory through exercising dominion.

Despite this setback, God's redemptive plan unfolds through His Son, Jesus Christ. Through His sacrificial work, Jesus restores our authority and empowers us to reclaim our rightful dominion. Each day presents an opportunity for us to actively engage in this divine mission, confronting the forces that oppose God's purposes. We obtain the power to accomplish this task by reading His word, seeking His guidance through the Holy Spirit, and following the steps set before us. As children of the Most High God, we must strive daily to bring the kingdom of God to earth.

I have found that I am able to establish dominion through my show "What Would Kay Say?" As I prepare my message, my communication with God through prayer keeps me connected to the vine and produces fruit. This fruit is needed to show kindness to a hurting heart or speak a word of encouragement to someone in doubt. My fruit has opened doors that only God could open, keeping me from temptation, while allowing me the ability to conquer territory that is in desperate need of God's peaceful light.

Dominion, therefore, is not a passive privilege but an active responsibility. Through the transformative power of Christ and the indwelling of the Holy Spirit, we are equipped to manifest the glory of God in our lives and communities, bringing His kingdom to fruition here on earth.

Then God blessed them, and God
said to them, "Be fruitful and
multiply; fill the earth and subdue
it; have dominion over the fish of
the sea, over the birds of the air,
and over every living thing that
moves on the earth.

Genesis 1:28 (NKJV)

REFLECT ON THE WORD

How has God given you dominion over territory for the kingdom?

What areas in your life do you have to take dominion over?

How do you know that you are walking in dominion?

PRAYER

Lord,

As I navigate this earthly journey within the time allotted by You, help me to replicate Your kingdom here on earth. You gave us control from the beginning, and Christ came to show us how to accomplish this. Let my fruit demonstrate Your love, grace, and mercy so that all will want to know the God that I serve. I seek Your direction and guidance when I don't know how to escape the snare of the enemy.

In Jesus' name,

Amen.

We are His cherished children.

MOTIVATED
BY THE
WORD

6

TRANSFORMATIVE GRACE
THROUGH REPOSITIONING
RESET

(v) set again or differently

The concept of reset denotes the act of setting things differently. It beautifully resonates with the gracious character of our God. Every day, His faithfulness grants us the gift of a new beginning. The word reset encapsulates the endless opportunities God provides for us. His boundless love offers us second, third, fourth, and infinite chances to realign our lives.

Having endured an unhappy marriage for years, coupled with the responsibility of raising two boys that were not biologically my own, threw me into a state of fear and desperation. After being in the marriage for so long, the thought of leaving the relationship and being on my own was frightening. I had become jaded by the pain life had brought to me when circumstances didn't turn out as planned. How could I ever trust my heart to another; especially when this relationship was born in church. We were in ministry together; I never expected this outcome.

How could this be? I prayed for the marriage to work, but in life, God will never force decisions upon you. He will always respect your freedom of choice. In a marriage, joined together by God, it still takes both parties to agree to stay as one. Regardless of one's spiritual training, you cannot control the will of another's heart. When it didn't work out, I looked to God to reset my life. The beauty of reset is that grace allows the opportunity to make right what turned out wrong.

God can create beauty from ashes, replace what was stolen, and reclaim our lost time. That was all I had to hold onto as I found myself on my own. Looking for another opportunity to live for God and complete my journey, God heard my cries and answered my prayers.

Through everything we experience God holds onto us. We are His cherished children. If you're yearning to reset your life, seeking more time to get things right, open your heart to God's grace. Welcome the renewed mercies, allowing them to guide you on your journey of purpose.

Through the Lord's mercies we
are not consumed, Because His
compassions fail not. They are
new every morning; Great is Your
faithfulness.

Lamentations 3:22-23 (NKJV)

REFLECT ON THE WORD

How do you plan to utilize the reset given to you for your life's circumstances?

What circumstances led you to that point?

How do you perceive God's role in your life when things don't turn out as you planned or hoped?

PRAYER

God,

In the name of Jesus, I ask to be continually reminded of the daily opportunities granted through Your grace and mercy. May I always recognize and embrace the second chances to do the right thing. You granted us grace to live through sin, not to continue to live in sin. Grace is our reset button. Let me press upon it daily.

In Jesus' name,

Amen.

But why is this so hard to do?

MOTIVATED
BY THE
WORD

7

THE PATH TO GOD'S PROMISES
OBEDIENT

(adj.) complying or willing to comply with orders or request; submissive to another's will

The concept of being obedient is deeply intertwined with God's promises, assuring that His spoken word will always be fulfilled. For those who choose to obey, this serves as a source of hope and confidence; His promises are steadfast and reliable. Throughout scripture, God has provided numerous assurances of His faithfulness and the life that His Word brings to His believers.

But why is this so hard to do?

As I pondered the concept of obedience and how true God is to His word, I wonder why we find it so hard to be obedient. We see this exemplified over and over throughout the scriptures—from Adam and Eve to Sodom and Gomorrah in the Book of Genesis, from Samson in the Book of Judges to the Seven Churches in the Book of Revelation.

There have been times in my life that I too have struggled with the concept of being obedient. Whether it's not following the Spirit or blatantly being defiant, I still struggle. What harm will another slice of cake do? It's only a glass of wine with dinner; what harm can it cause? They both provide a temporary form of comfort, yet neither are good for me. Romans 14 tells us that we will all have to give an account for ourselves and to not become a stumbling block for someone else.

In spite of how we may feel, there are grave consequences for disobedience. Someone's life hangs in the balance; it is not always about you! While obedience may present challenges, for those who love the Lord, obedience becomes a joyful and fulfilling path. It grants access to everything that we need.

If you are willing and obedient,
You shall eat the good of the land

Isaiah 1:19 (NKJV)

REFLECT ON THE WORD

In what areas of your life are you struggling with being obedient?

How have you been able to overcome it?

Have you experienced a difference in your life by being obedient?

PRAYER

Lord,

I express my gratitude for the prosperity that obedience brings, acknowledging that without You, I am nothing. As we reason together, I humbly ask You to cleanse my sins and make them as white as snow. My heart is receptive to Your will, and I stand ready to walk according to Your word.

In Jesus' name,

Amen.

*Through the cross, we have been freed
from the burden of sin.*

MOTIVATED
BY THE
WORD

8

LIVING THE ABUNDANT LIFE WITH JESUS
FREEDOM

*(n) the power or right to act, speak or think as one wants
without hindrance or restraint*

There exists a profound freedom that surpasses
earthly limitations—a freedom bestowed upon us
by Jesus Christ Himself. As citizens of the United
States, we often overlook the remarkable liberties
we enjoy, such as the freedom to worship and
express ourselves. Sadly, many around the world
do not share these privileges. However, they can
still experience the unparalleled freedom offered
by Jesus Christ. His sacrifice on the cross paved
the way for a freedom unlike any other,
transcending worldly constraints.

Through the cross, we have been freed from
the burden of sin. We have become new
creations, given another chance to live out our
God-given purpose. Christ made it available to us

all, but we have to take it. We have to accept it and embrace it with everything we have.

Although there have been times in my life when I found it difficult to hold on to the notion that I was actually free, I remember being pregnant with my son in a time when being a single mother was still frowned upon. It was the Eighties, and there were some in Corporate America who still held on to the notion that a woman had to be married to have a child. I was well acquainted with discrimination, but I was better acquainted with the scripture that my spirit held fast to—"there is no condemnation for those who are in Christ Jesus" (Romans 8:1).

As believers, we are called to embrace freedom and live according to His promises, which are unmatched by anything the world has to offer. Remember and cherish the extraordinary freedom granted to us by our Savior.

Therefore if the Son makes you free,
you shall be free indeed.

John 8:36 (NKJV)

REFLECT ON THE WORD

Reflect on a time in your life where you have been made to feel less than the promise that God has given to you.

How has holding on to what God says about you allowed you to walk in your freedom?

How did you handle it?

PRAYER

Lord,

Help me never to take for granted the privileges bestowed upon me as Your child. I have the freedom to worship You whenever I please, and I will forever give You praise. I pray that I abide in Your word, putting into practice all of Your promises. May Your truth set me free each day. I am grateful for the blessings You have given me, and I trust in Your promises.

In Jesus' name,

Amen.

...True transformation requires more than just surface level adjustments.

MOTIVATED
BY THE
WORD

9

THE TRANSFORMATIVE
TEACHINGS OF CHRIST
REFORM

*(v) make changes in (something, typically a social, political,
or economic institutions or practice) in order to improve it*

Making substantive changes to enhance a
situation or practice—this is what happened when
Jesus entered the world. His earthly ministry
ushered in a transformative reform that surpassed
behavioral adjustments—it was a revival of hearts
and minds. Jesus declared that He came not to
change the law but to fulfill it. His mission was to
rescue humanity from eternal condemnation by
fulfilling the law and bearing the consequences of
our sins.

Through His teachings, Christ illuminates the
path to living in harmony with God's will. He
urges us to undergo internal changes that lead to a
more fulfilling life. Just as in His time here on
earth, we still have an issue with change. No one

likes change, even if it is for the better. Our brains are not accustomed to moving out of our comfort zone. We are creatures of habit; if it's not broken, don't fix it! That is what the kingdom of God is all about: making us adapt to change. We were broken and would never have been granted the opportunity to enter into heaven without the help of Jesus. He came into a broken world to fix what we were incapable of fixing—ourselves.

I remember a time when I struggled with a significant change in my own life. I had been laid off from the only career that I had ever known - working in the financial industry. Adapting to a new position in a new industry, telecommunication, presented so many challenges at first. During that time, I realized that true transformation required more than just surface-level adjustments. It demanded a change in my heart and mind, much like the profound changes Jesus calls us to make.

His miraculous works of healing, from the man afflicted with leprosy and the woman with the issue of blood, to raising Lazarus from the dead, all showcased His power to restore and renew. When we embrace reform inspired by the teachings of Jesus Christ, it is more than just making surface-level changes—it is a profound transformation of our hearts and minds. As we align ourselves with God's divine will, we draw nearer to His perfect design for our lives.

Knowing that a man is not justified
by the works of the law but by
faith in Jesus Christ, even we have
believed in Christ Jesus, that we
might be justified by faith in Christ
and not by the works of the law; for
by the works of the law no flesh shall
be justified.

Galatians 2:16 (NKJV)

REFLECT ON THE WORD

How has serving the kingdom changed your outlook on the world and social issues?

What part do you play in the bigger picture to effect change?

How do you handle change within your life?

PRAYER

Lord,

Your Word encourages me not to conform to the ways of this world but to be transformed by the renewing of my mind. Grant me the strength and guidance to embrace the process of change, one step at a time, so that I may reform myself according to Your good, acceptable, and perfect will. Thank you for illuminating the path to eternal life through Your teachings.

In Jesus' name,

Amen.

10

ACCEPTING THE CALL OF GOD
COMMIT

*(v) pledge or bind (a person or an organization) to a
certain course or policy*

Discipleship is not for the faint of heart, so it
stands to reason that embarking on the journey of
discipleship is no small feat. It requires courage,
determination, and a steadfast commitment to
follow the path laid out before us. Like Jonah,
who initially shied away from his divine calling, I
too found myself grappling with the weight of
commitment in my early years as a believer.

However, through the examples of faithful
servants like the Apostle Paul, I've come to
understand the profound significance of
unwavering dedication to God's will. Paul's
declaration, 'To live is Christ, to die is gain,'
encapsulates the essence of true commitment.

Despite the uncertainties and challenges of life, Paul remained resolute in his commitment to preach the gospel and fulfill God's purpose.

As followers of Christ, we are called to emulate this unwavering commitment, trusting in God's promises and surrendering our lives completely to His will. Commitment becomes our guiding light, steering us daily towards the fulfillment of God's plan and the realization of His blessings in our lives. Reflecting on my journey of commitment to the Lord, I am reminded of the profound truth that sincere surrender is not without its challenges. Finding myself on a path similar to that of Jonah, I knew that I had a message to give but wanted to deliver it another way. I wanted to "do" God when it was convenient for me, when God fit into my plans. That is not how God works, yet we still try to fit Him into a box and open only when needed. In the end, my plans were not working as I had pictured, so I decided that obedience is better than sacrifice.

In my commitment to God I found true fulfillment and purpose. My total surrender allowed Him to show me what was best for me and where He wanted me to be: on the radio speaking into the lives of many. Let us, therefore, recommit ourselves daily to His will, trusting in His faithfulness to bring about His plans in our lives. May our commitment to God be a testament to His goodness and grace, inspiring others to embark on their own journey of surrender and devotion.

.

Commit your way to the Lord,
trust also in Him,
and He shall bring it to pass.

Psalm 37:5 (NKJV)

REFLECT ON THE WORD

Are you struggling with the notion of being committed to God?

What do you think will happen when you fully commit to the Lord?

What helps you remain committed when you are unsure if you are doing what God has called you to do?

PRAYER

Father,

As I look to follow Your commands and engage my heart to follow Your will, help me in my walk to complete all that You would have me to do. Your word says that You will bring the works of my hand to pass if I submit myself to You. Here I am, willing and able, Lord.

In Jesus' name,

Amen.

11

THE POWER OF STAYING CENTERED
FOCUS

(n) the center of interest or activity

It's essential to reevaluate our approach to tasks and priorities, especially when it comes to maintaining our focus on what truly matters. In today's fast-paced world, the concept of multitasking has become increasingly prevalent. However, as technology has evolved, so too have our understandings of productivity and efficiency. Multitasking may seem like an efficient way to tackle multiple tasks simultaneously, but studies have shown that the brain's attention is primarily focused on one task at a time. Similarly, in our spiritual lives, maintaining a singular focus on God is paramount.

When God created us, He never intended for us to do several things at one time. He wanted us to keep our main focus on Him. When we keep Him first in our lives, we accomplish all that He created us to do. Every decision concerning our lives needs to be discussed with our Heavenly Father. I believed God when He said that I should leave my career and pursue my calling. Easier said than done. Was He aware that He had positioned me into a cushy six-figure income that I had become quite accustomed to? From the palace to the pit? Lord, I was moving backwards, or so I thought.

Looking to maintain my lifestyle, I took on another position as an Enrollment Advisor, reasoning with God that it was for a good cause—I was helping young ladies make life-altering decisions. We can never multitask God into our everyday work tasks or life situations. Our main focus should always remain on Him first. Just as the scripture commands us to have no other gods before Him, they also assure us that perfect peace comes to those whose minds are focused on God.

I couldn't keep up with counseling, writing, the radio show, and life—something had to give. In His infinite wisdom, God reminded me to be still because true peace and fulfillment come from maintaining our focus on Him. Let us prioritize our relationship with God above all else, trusting in His guidance and provision in every aspect of our lives.

You will keep him in perfect peace,
Whose mind is stayed on You.

Isaiah 26:3 (NKJV)

REFLECT ON THE WORD

Have you ever tried to assist God with the "steps" He has for your life?

What lessons were learned from giving God a hand?

How do you handle multitasking various parts of your life?

PRAYER

Heavenly Father,

In a world filled with distractions and competing priorities, please help me keep my focus on You above all else. Grant me the wisdom to recognize when my attention is divided, and the strength to realign my priorities according to Your will. May my heart and mind be steadfastly fixed on You, day and night, as I navigate life's challenges and joys.

In Jesus' name,

Amen.

12

ANCHORED IN HIS WORD
HOPE

(n) a feeling of expectation and desire for a certain thing to happen

Hope is the anchor of our souls, the beacon that guides us through life's storms. It's been said that when hope fades, life loses its purpose. Yet, as believers, hope is not merely a wishful thought; it's the confident expectation that God is faithful to His promises. In the darkest moments, hope reminds us that dawn will break, and joy will come in the morning. It's the assurance that God's plans for us are good, filled with hope and a future. Even when circumstances seem bleak, hope keeps us steady, knowing that God is working all things together for our good.

With hope, we rise each morning, knowing that God's mercies are new every day. We face challenges with courage, believing that God is with us, guiding and sustaining us. Hope whispers to our hearts that no matter how dire the situation, God's love never fails, and His faithfulness endures forever. I hung onto those words like an acrobat to a trapeze. Hope has always been a principal aspect of my journey. Without it, I could not have continued forward. How was I going to live? How was I going to pay bills? All I had to do was follow the call, right?

So I obeyed and found myself placed into the wilderness. Visions of Jesus flashed through my mind after He was baptized in the Jordan River by John the Baptist. Jesus, ready to walk into His purpose, embracing all that God had given to Him, still found Himself dealing with an enemy on an empty stomach! This solidified in my mind that moving with the timing of God does not guarantee smooth sailing. We have to have hope, trusting and believing that things will get better.

When we hold onto hope tightly, it centers us and keeps us grounded where all of our dreams, goals, and God's blessings are located. It fills us with courage, strengthens our faith, and leads us into the abundant life God has promised. In every trial, there will be triumph, but we have to stay the course. We have to allow hope to be our constant companion, reminding us that with God, all things are possible.

Now may the God of hope fill you
with all joy and peace in believing,
that you may abound in hope by the
power of the Holy Spirit.

Romans 15:13 (NKJV)

REFLECT ON THE WORD

How do you balance holding onto hope while also dealing with the reality of current challenges?

How can you actively cultivate hope in your daily life and encourage others to do the same?

Can you recall a specific moment when hope guided you through a particularly tough situation?

PRAYER

Lord,

I hold on to the hope that You have placed within my heart—hope of a better life, hope of a better future, hope in Your son Jesus Christ, our hope of glory. It is through Him that I have secured eternal life with You and have a place in heaven. I have peace knowing that I can rest in Him and that I have the presence of the Holy Spirit guiding me every day in every way.

In Jesus' name.

Amen

In a world filled with uncertainty and doubt, God's Word stands as truth and hope.

MOTIVATED
BY THE
WORD

13

THERE IS POWER IN THE WORD
BELIEVE

(v) accept (something) as true; feel sure of the truth of

God's Word is not merely a collection of letters and sounds; it is His divine will and purpose. To believe in God's Word is to believe in His Son, Jesus Christ, who came to dwell among us, full of grace and truth. Through Jesus, we find redemption, salvation, and eternal life. He is the fulfillment of all God's promises, His love, and His mercy. When we affirm our belief in God's Word, we are embracing the very essence of God Himself. We are affirming our trust in His sovereignty, our confidence in His goodness, and our hope in His promises.

In a world filled with uncertainty and doubt, God's Word stands as truth and hope. It is a firm foundation upon which we can build our lives and anchor our faith. As we journey through life holding fast to God's Word, we know we will find truth, purpose, and ultimate fulfillment.

Education has always been a cornerstone in my family. I remember hearing, "No one can ever take away your knowledge," so it was important to ensure my son received the best education available. His formative years began in private institutions. When he was entering 6th grade, I decided to place him in the gifted and talented classes at the local public school. He met the academic qualifications, surpassing their requirements. However, they refused to enter him into the program on a technicality—he had not attended pre-K in that school system. I was appalled. This had to be a mistake.

Knowing what the blood of Jesus stands for, I decided to challenge the system. When you know the God who controls all things, even the smallest amount of faith—the size of a mustard seed—can move mountains. I stood on God's words: "Ask, and it shall be given unto you." I held onto what He said, believing in the power behind it. Simply put, I believed in God, and He delivered.

But without faith it is impossible to please Him, for he who comes to God must believe that He is, and that He is a rewarder of those who diligently seek Him.

Hebrews 11:6 (NKJV)

REFLECT ON THE WORD

What are you believing God for?

When was the last time you prayed believing by faith that God would deliver what you wanted?

How do you balance worldly knowledge with the wisdom that comes from believing in God's word?

PRAYER

As a human, Lord,

I am programmed to believe only what my five senses tell me to be true. It has been said that it is impossible to please You without having faith. But one can only have faith if they believe in a thing. Today Lord, I open my heart to every promise, every word spoken over my life, and what is written in Your book. Lord, I believe in You and Your Son, Jesus Christ. Without Him, I am nothing; with Him, I can do anything. Lord, my prayer is that You continue to show me how to trust in You, especially when I find it impossible to believe.

In Jesus' name,

Amen.

The enemy will always try to remove any blessings that God has given you.

MOTIVATED
BY THE
WORD

14

GOD'S WORD IS A SHIELD
TRUTH

(n) that which is true or in accordance with fact or reality.

When a story is being told, it's often said that there are three parts: your part, my part, and the truth. Since the beginning, Satan has sought to distort the ultimate truth: the word of God. Even when we're fully aware of what is true, we can be deceived if we're caught off guard. This is what happened to Eve in the garden.

We must be vigilant in not allowing our point of view to align with the world's version of truth. Doing this leaves us vulnerable to false information and the establishment of idolatry. The only truth we should hold in our hearts is the word of God, as it alone has the power to bring about transformation in our lives. Everything else is merely opinion.

It has been said that pride comes before the fall. This is what happened in the kingdom of God—Lucifer allowed his pride to take over and cause him to lose his prominent position in God's kingdom. We, being children of the Most High, should never allow the word of men to cloud what we know to be true.

I experienced this firsthand in my career. Moving up the corporate ladder quickly in the financial business caught the eyes of executives and started some to question how this could be possible. A young African American female moving up the ranks in this Caucasian male-dominated field of finance—what gives?

The enemy will always try to remove any blessings that God has given to you. I was reassigned to a new manager who demoted me, stating that I, by his standards, did not possess the qualifications he wanted for the position. He also claimed credit for anything I had accomplished while being under his supervision. When asked in my year review how I was coping with my new position, I stated to the VP, Senior Manager, and HR, that I obtained my status within the company through hard work and my faith. If they wanted to keep me from moving into any other positions, that was fine with me—it meant that God had something better for me. My trust in God was more powerful than any position available for me.

This experience taught me to rely completely on God's truth rather than the shifting opinions of others. It reaffirmed my belief that God's word is the ultimate truth, guiding and sustaining me through any trial.

Lead me in Your truth and teach me, For You are the God of my salvation; On You I wait all the day.

Psalm 25:5 (NKJV)

REFLECT ON THE WORD

How do you discern the truth from falsehoods in your daily life?

Can you identify a time when you relied on God's truth to navigate through a challenging situation?

What steps can you take to ensure you remain focused on God's truth rather than being swayed by the world's version of truth?

PRAYER

God,

My flesh wants what it wants, even though it knows that it is contrary to what You want for me. Holy Spirit, I ask that You continue to guide me in all things true, all things holy, and all things of God. Lord, Your word I have written upon my heart. I will use it to guide me into all truth for today and evermore. Thank You, Lord, for Your guidance and wisdom.

In Jesus' name.

Amen.

15

THE PATH TO PERSONAL GROWTH
ACCOUNTABLE

(adj.) (Of a person, organization, or institution) required or expected to justify actions or decisions; responsible.

"Cancel culture" is the predominant force in today's society. It dictates an environment where openly acknowledging imperfections has become increasingly uncommon. The fear of deviating from societal norms or facing rejection often prevents individuals from embracing their flaws openly. This reluctance to admit faults is reminiscent of many historical events. For instance, Pilate's decision to release Barabbas instead of Jesus, where self-preservation and societal pressures outweighed moral accountability. This comparison underscores the ongoing challenge for individuals to confront their shortcomings and embrace personal growth.

Jesus told us in Matthew 9:13 that He did not come for the righteous, but for the sinner to repent. If we shy away from acknowledging our flaws and speaking up when needed, how can we expect to receive the blessings and anointing that God has in store for us?

Being a Christian requires faith in God and not in oneself. The only way for me to walk in the calling placed on my life is to allow the Holy Spirit to hold me responsible for my actions and the words that come out of my mouth. I once heard a lawyer say ignorance is no excuse for breaking the law. I too have to remember that in order to live life as God intended me to, I have to know His word and follow the instructions I've been given. There is a true test to hold oneself accountable; I call it the mirror test. If, when you look in the mirror, you like *who* you see, you've passed the test.

Jesus said to them, "If you were blind, you would have no sin; but now you say, 'We see.' Therefore your sin remains."

John 9:41 (NKJV)

REFLECT ON THE WORD

Can you think of a time when societal pressure influenced you to deny or hide your faith or beliefs?

How did it make you feel afterward? How can you ensure that you are living in accordance with God's word and instructions?

What practical steps can you take to improve in this area?

PRAYER

In my failure to take responsibility for my actions, Lord, I humbly ask for Your forgiveness. Open my eyes to see where I have strayed from Your will and neglected Your instructions for my life. I confess that I have been consumed by my own desires, making it difficult for me to acknowledge my disobedience. Please cleanse my heart and purify my hands so that I may serve You faithfully.

In Jesus' name,

Amen.

*...I felt a nudge to mention church,
but I chose to stay silent.*

MOTIVATED
BY THE
WORD

16

AUTHENTICITY FOR THE KINGDOM
DISINGENUOUS

(adj) Not candid or sincere, typically by pretending that one knows less about something than one really does.

We have been called to such a time as this. Each of us is placed by God in this specific moment to make a significant impact for His kingdom. Regrettably, many Christians shy away from sharing their faith, are hesitant to share the gospel, or stand up for what is right. Instead, we often choose to remain anonymous in our beliefs, fearing judgment or rejection from others.

Peter, accused of being a follower of the Messiah, vehemently denied knowing Jesus. Ironically, Jesus warned Peter of his actions, stating that it would happen before the rooster crowed three times. This should serve as a reminder that despite what we think or believe, God knows all. That same truth is present today. Jesus cautioned us against insincerity; if we deny

Him before others, He will likewise deny us before the Father. In the grand scheme, our allegiance to our Lord and Savior eclipses the importance of human opinions.

I remember a time early in my walk when I was hesitant to share my faith with a group of friends that I hung out with. They asked me about my weekend plans, and I felt a nudge to mention church, but I chose to stay silent. Later, I felt convicted about not seizing the opportunity to witness. This experience reminded me of Peter's denial and the importance of being bold and sincere in my faith. It also shed light on the company that I was keeping. I realized I should always be able to share my faith with whomever I am around. I am grateful to say that I no longer struggle with this issue.

But whoever denies Me before men,
him I will also deny before My
Father who is in heaven.

Matthew 10:33 (NKJV)

REFLECT ON THE WORD

Have you ever felt hesitant to share your faith or stand up for what you believe is right?

What were your fears?

In what ways can you strengthen your allegiance to Jesus over the opinions of others?

PRAYER

Heavenly Father,

Grant me opportunities to boldly share the gospel with those who need it. Guide me to individuals ready to receive Your Son, that they may know salvation. Empower me to faithfully fulfill the Great Commission, spreading Your word with diligence and truth.

In Jesus' name,

Amen

His love for us is intrinsic
to His nature…

MOTIVATED
BY THE
WORD

17

THE REDEEMING GRACE OF GOD'S LOVE
JUSTIFICATION

(n) the action of showing something to be right or reasonable.

In Theology, the action of declaring or making righteous in the sight of God

When we contemplate measuring our actions against God's expectations, it surpasses our understanding. Often, we equate our actions with achieving status or merit. Yet, all glory belongs to the Almighty. His love transcends our deeds and efforts. His love for us is intrinsic to His nature, bestowed upon us as His creation. We are Imago Dei, made in His image and for His purpose. When God sought to reconcile us to Himself, He sent His Son, demonstrating His boundless love.

I continually marvel at why God loves me despite my imperfections. There are times I disappoint Him, unintentionally allowing my flesh to hinder my walk. Remembering as Paul stated, what I am supposed to do I don't—-but what I am not supposed to do I do! So, because of my disobedience, I am profoundly grateful for Jesus' sacrifice on the cross. Through Him, we receive countless chances. When Jesus took on our sins, offering us His righteousness, He exchanged our condemnation for justification, restoring communion with God.

Therefore, as through one man's offense judgment came to all men, resulting in condemnation, even so through one Man's righteous act the free gift came to all men, resulting in justification of life.

Romans 5:18 (NKJV)

REFLECT ON THE WORD

How does justification through Jesus' sacrifice resonate with your own journey of faith?

What are some specific ways you can honor God and reflect His kingdom in your actions and decisions?

How has grace played a role in your life as a believer?

PRAYER

Lord,

I am forever grateful for the sacrifice of Your Son, Jesus Christ. Through His blood, I am redeemed and justified, granted new life. Help me daily to remember the purpose You have ordained for my life. May everything I do bring honor and glory to Your name, reflecting Your kingdom rather than my own desires. In Your Son's work, I find complete salvation, for which I am eternally thankful.

In Jesus' name,

Amen.

Can the dry places in our lives be restored?

MOTIVATED
BY THE
WORD

18

FINDING NEW LIFE IN
RESTORATION
REVIVE

(v) To restore to consciousness or life

In the book of Ezekiel, God posed a profound question to the prophet: Can these dry bones live? Despite God's omniscience, the question perplexed Ezekiel. Today, God poses the same question to us: Can the dry places in our lives be restored? Are we willing to invite Him into those hidden areas of our hearts? Only we can answer that question, though God already knows our response.

There was a time in my life when I was walking the middle of the road. I had one foot in the church and one foot in the world. When I first said that out loud, it was hard to believe. After all the blessings God had given me—the ability to graduate college, maintain a full time position in the financial industry—all while raising my son. Even though I was able to see His hand on my life, I was still afraid to totally surrender myself to Him, always thinking that my total obedience would result in my missing out on something.

Looking back at that time in my life, God was longing to manifest new life within me. He is looking to manifest new life in all of us, but it requires our repentance and seeking forgiveness. It also requires us to surrender who we are to who He wants us to be. Like Ezekiel witnessed the bones coming to life at God's command, God wants to and can revive our dryness and bring new life to our souls.

I will put My Spirit in you, and you
shall live, and I will place you in
your own land. Then you shall know
that I, the LORD, have spoken it
and performed it, says the LORD.

Ezekiel 37:14 (NKJV)

REFLECT ON THE WORD

How does Ezekiel's vision of dry bones coming to life resonate with your own experiences of spiritual renewal and revival?

What specific areas of your life do you need to surrender more fully to God to experience His revival and restoration?

How can you share the message of God's revival and restoration with others who may be experiencing dryness or spiritual weariness?

PRAYER

Lord,

As You breathe into me, revive all the dry places within my life, even those I've forgotten. You alone know my heart, and only You can see what I truly need. With just one word from You, my dry bones will come alive again. Restore me to the purpose You ordained for me from my very foundation. I am ready to be filled with Your Spirit, knowing that it brings life, joy, and peace. Thank you, God, for reviving my dry bones.

In Jesus' name,

Amen

...God's truth allows us to hold on to promises that He has given us.

MOTIVATED
BY THE
WORD

19

STANDING UNMOVABLE ON THE PROMISES
STEADFAST

(adj) resolutely or dutifully firm and unwavering

Have you ever watched a cat fixated on its prey, eyes locked in unwavering focus, body poised for action? It's a mesmerizing sight, one that speaks volumes about the power of single-minded determination. In many ways, God calls us to embody that same steadfastness in our faith. Like the cat resolutely stalking its prey, we are called to be resolute in our beliefs, grounded firmly in the unchanging truth of God's word. It's about being unmovable and unhindered, even in the face of life's many distractions and challenges.

In the spring of 2015 my mom became ill with blood poisoning. Sepsis, as it is known in the medical field, kills 1 out of every 5 patients who have been diagnosed with the illness. I can recall going to the hospital every day to sit with her while she underwent treatments for the infection that was raging through her body. Sitting by her bedside my fervent prayer was fueled by our Comforter, the Holy Spirit. He reminded me to remain unwavering and take God at His word; by his stripes we are healed. Glory be to the father; she was not the one of the five.

When we remain steadfast in our faith, we become powerful witnesses for the gospel. Just as a cat's focus never wavers from its target, our commitment to God's truth allows us to hold on to promises that He has given us. This in turn assists us in effectively sharing His love and message of salvation with others. In a world filled with uncertainty and doubt, our steadfast faith becomes a beacon of hope and truth. It's a testament to the unchanging nature of God's love and commitment to His people. And as we walk in that faith, we can trust that God will use us to illuminate the lives of those around us, drawing them closer to Him.

Therefore know that the LORD your God, He is God, the faithful God who keeps covenant and mercy for a thousand generations with those who love Him and keep His commandments.

Deuteronomy 7:9 (NKJV)

REFLECT ON THE WORD

What personal challenges have tested your faith, and how did you remain steadfast during those times?

What does Deuteronomy 7:9 teach you about God's faithfulness and commitment to His people?

In what ways can you apply the lesson of being steadfast in your daily life and faith journey?

PRAYER

Lord, my earnest prayer is to dwell continually in Your presence. May I immerse myself in Your word, inscribing every promise upon my heart, that my life may radiate Your goodness. With the guidance of the Holy Spirit, I will stand firm and unwavering in all that I do. I anchor myself in Your truth, believing every word written and spoken by You, O Lord.

In Jesus' name,

Amen.

God's presence is our greatest weapon.

MOTIVATED
BY THE
WORD

20

A SOLDIER IN THE ARMY OF THE LORD
CONQUEROR

(n) one who conquerors; one who wins a country in war, subdues or subjugates a people or overcomes an adversary.

The scriptures vividly illustrate the incredible power we possess when we align ourselves with God. They remind us that with Him on our side, no force in the universe can stand against us. We're not just ordinary individuals; we're empowered warriors, armed with the strength of the Almighty. God's presence is our greatest weapon, ready to wage war on our behalf against the darkest forces of this world. With Him leading the charge, we're equipped to tear down strongholds and face any challenge with unwavering courage.

Honestly speaking, I don't feel like a conqueror on the days when life decides to throw a curveball when I least expect it. The pressure from work, school, and family—life in general can become overwhelming making it difficult to see my way through. It's during these times my mind reflects on King David in 1 Samuel 30:8 where the scriptures tell us David encouraged himself in the Lord his God. We have to encourage ourselves, and remind ourselves that we are more than conquerors through Christ Jesus.

Clad in the full armor of God, we press on, heads held high, undeterred by the trials and tribulations that come our way. Our victory isn't just a possibility; it's a certainty, secured by the precious blood of Jesus Christ shed on the cross. It's a victory that transcends even death itself.

Today, as we revel in the promise of eternal life with our heavenly Father, let us rejoice in the unshakable assurance that comes from knowing we are more than conquerors through Him who loves us.

Yet in all these things we are more than conquerors through Him who loved us.

Romans 8:37 (NKJV)

REFLECT ON THE WORD

Can you recall a specific time in your life when you felt overwhelmed but found strength and encouragement in God? How did that experience shape your faith?

What does it mean to you personally to be more than a conqueror through Christ?

How does this identity influence your daily life and decisions?

PRAYER

Lord, through His sacrifice on the cross, Jesus has bestowed upon me the mantle of a conqueror. No force can overpower me or diminish my worth, for I am a cherished child of the Most High God. Guided by the Holy Spirit, I walk in divine strength every day. With God by my side, I am capable of achieving all things and expanding the territory of His kingdom. Thank you, Lord, for your unwavering presence and support.

In Jesus' name,

Amen.

*Exhibiting patience
in chaotic situations.*

MOTIVATED
BY THE
WORD

21

LIVING LIFE IN THE TRUTH
AUTHENTIC

(adj.) of undisputed origin; genuine

In today's social media environment, authenticity is often a clarion cry of influencers as they share insights into their genuine selves. But what does it truly mean to be authentic? If you follow social media, having authenticity can come in many different ways. It can be sharing a doctor's prognosis of a terminal illness. It can be revealing your grandmother's secret recipe that has been passed down from generation to generation. To most it means sharing everything going on in your life with the public at all times.

There are times that I straddle the fence when it comes to being authentic in today's world. When speaking on the air, I have to ask myself the question: am I sharing too much information, or am I not sharing enough? We all have a testimony as we're walking this journey of life. Our testimonies are supposed to encourage others that are going through the same experiences, showing how God can make a way. I have learned that if you intend to show your true authentic self, make sure you are standing on the Word of the Lord.

As Christians, authenticity takes on an entirely different meaning. Being authentic means mirroring the examples set by Jesus in our daily lives through continuous manifestations of the fruits of the spirit. That would include having a positive attitude during difficult times. Expressions of goodwill without looking for something in return. Exhibiting patience in chaotic situations. It entails following His teachings as outlined in the Bible: loving God wholeheartedly, loving others as we love ourselves, and extending forgiveness as needed. Only when our lives coincide with these principles can we genuinely claim to be followers of the gospel, looking in expectation to the promises and blessings from the Lord.

He who speaks truth
declares righteousness,
But a false witness, deceit.

Proverbs 12:17 (NKJV)

REFLECT ON THE WORD

How do the teachings of Jesus and the Bible guide your understanding of authenticity?

What specific scriptures inspire you to live authentically? How do you define authenticity in your own life?

What steps can you take to ensure your actions align with this definition?

PRAYER

Heavenly Father,

I have hidden Your word in my heart, enabling me to speak Your truth boldly in every situation. Grant me the courage to speak unapologetically, allowing Your words to flow through me and impact lives. Your truth sets us free and leads to abundant life, a gift made possible through Jesus. Thank You for Your boundless love, grace, and mercy.

In Jesus' name,

Amen.

*Peter and John performed a miracle at
the gate called Beautiful.*

MOTIVATED
BY THE
WORD

22

GOD'S PLAN FOR CHANGE
ADAPT

(v) make something suitable for a new use or purpose; modify

The creation of the World Wide Web transformed the way we previously sought knowledge. It replaced traditional methods, such as going to libraries, with the instantaneous access provided by personal computers. Though it seemed overwhelming at first, this transition allowed us to quickly adapt to a new era of information accessibility.

The 12 disciples faced a similar challenge when they encountered Jesus and He introduced them to His method of teaching the word. His approach differed from the conventional practices of the synagogue. In fact, everything that Jesus did forced the people of Israel to adapt to a new way of thinking and a new way of looking at God's word. Never again would they be satisfied with reading the scrolls without invoking action. Could a lame man who had been crippled from birth walk? He most certainly could! Peter and John performed a miracle at the gate called Beautiful. The book of Acts tells us that they spoke "In the name of Jesus Christ of Nazareth, rise up and walk," demonstrating how speaking the word of God in Jesus' name brought life.

I too have had instances in my life where I had to adapt to a new way of thinking. Growing up and attending church 30 years ago looks a lot different than it does now. Back then, the congregation, me included, looked to its leaders for direction and guidance. But that is not what church was supposed to be about. Like the disciples, I have learned that following religion with its man-made rules and regulations is not what God intended for us. When Christ came, it was so that we could reestablish a relationship with the Father—not one made up of mandatory gatherings on first Sundays, but a real connection. One that could only be achieved through reading His word and spending time in His presence.

Despite the initial difficulty in adjusting to this new style of instruction, the disciples embraced Christ's teachings wholeheartedly and eventually became adept at sharing them with others. The same is true for us today; we must embrace the authority given to us through Jesus' sacrifice on the cross. Do you want to change your life and the lives of those around you? Speak His name. I stand on the truth that when we do this, we will perform even greater works than He did, by just speaking His name.

And do not be conformed to this
world, but be transformed by the
renewing of your mind, that you
may prove what is that good and
acceptable and perfect will of God.

Romans 12:1-2 (NKJV)

REFLECT ON THE WORD

In what areas of your spiritual journey do you find it most challenging to embrace change and new directions from God?

Can you recall a time when you had to adapt to a significant change in your life? How did you respond, and what was the outcome?

How has renewing your mind helped in your walk with the Lord?

PRAYER

Lord,

Grant me the humility and wisdom to embrace
the new directions You have ordained for my life.
Help me cultivate flexibility and openness to Your
guidance, even when it challenges my comfort
zone. Grant me the ability to discern and pursue
unfamiliar paths, knowing that they align with
Your divine purpose for me. May I shine as a
beacon of Your light in the world, reflecting Your
grace and truth to all.

In Jesus' name,

Amen.

23

MOTIVATED BY THE WORD
INSPIRE

(v) fill (someone) with the urge or ability to do or feel something, especially to do something creative.

All scripture carries the divine touch of God Himself. When we immerse ourselves in the Bible, we can trust that every word reflects God's intended message for His people. Consider the remarkable process where scribes, guided by the Holy Spirit, transcribed the words, "Thus says the Lord." Despite any doubts or uncertainties they may have had, they faithfully recorded the heavenly guidance they received. The narratives found within the Bible, including the Gospels penned by the disciples, offer unique perspectives on the life and teachings of Jesus. Just as eyewitnesses might recount an event with differing viewpoints, each author presents their unique outlook.

Our lives today also reflect God's ongoing inspiration. His words speak to us as we navigate a world filled with chaos and uncertainty, offering each of us the same outcome from a personal perspective. His healing for one person's cancer is the same as His comfort for another's anxiety or deliverance from depression. It has always been about His love, mercy, and grace freely given to each of us.

Regardless of the diverse accounts, the underlying message remains steadfast: God communicates clearly through His Word, incessantly guiding His people along His path. Throughout history, God has ensured that His written instructions endure, serving as an eternal compass for His people to follow.

Now may the God of patience and comfort grant you to be like-minded toward one another, according to Christ Jesus, that you may with one mind and one mouth glorify the God and Father of our Lord Jesus Christ.

Romans 15:5-6 (NKJV)

REFLECT ON THE WORD

How does your experience reading the Bible compare to the scribes guided by the Holy Spirit to write God's Word?

How do you see God's Word as a source of inspiration and guidance in your daily life, especially during uncertainty or challenge?

How can you maintain a consistent practice of allowing God's Word to sanctify you and empower you through His Holy Spirit, so that your life bears fruit that glorifies Him?

PRAYER

Lord,

May Your written Word inspire me to walk in the footsteps of Your Son, Jesus Christ, always in obedience and by faith. Guide me to treat others with love, kindness, and patience, mirroring Your own love for us. Let Your Word sanctify me and Your Holy Spirit empower me to bear fruit that glorifies Your Name.

In Jesus' name,

Amen.

The beauty of prayer lies
in its accessibility.

MOTIVATED
BY THE
WORD

24

MAINLINE THROUGH THE HOLY SPIRIT
PRAYER

(n) a solemn request for help or expression of thanks addressed to God or an object of worship.

Prayer serves as our direct line of communication with God, offering us the opportunity to speak with Him whenever we need. This spiritual language, established by God, allows us to freely express our thoughts, feelings, and desires to Him. While we can approach God with our needs, prayer is also a way for us to give Him praise and glorify His name.

Jesus understood our uncertainties about prayer and provided a model for us to follow. In the Book of Matthew, chapter 6, He taught us how to encompass every aspect of life in our conversations with God. Through the Lord's Prayer, we learn to approach God even when we don't know what to say, engaging in a dialogue of asking and listening. As we pray, we express our requests to our Heavenly Father in faith, trusting that He will answer according to His will.

The beauty of prayer lies in its accessibility. We don't need a specific posture or place for God to hear us. Personally, I've developed a daily habit of conversing with the Holy Spirit, sharing with Him all that unfolds in my life. Most of these conversations aren't about requests but about inviting Him into my decisions. This ongoing dialogue with God has proven deeply therapeutic.

Scripture reminds us that we often lack because we do not ask. God delights in communicating with His people, whether through signs, wonders, or answered prayers. When we maintain open lines of communication with Him, there is nothing He will withhold from us. All we need to do is ask, and God will respond with His abundant blessings.

And in that day you will ask Me nothing. Most assuredly, I say to you, whatever you ask the Father in My name He will give you.

John 16:23 (NKJV)

REFLECT ON THE WORD

How does prayer impact your daily life? Are there specific moments or routines where you find yourself most drawn to prayer?

In what ways do you incorporate praise and thanksgiving into your prayers?

PRAYER

Lord,

May my words and thoughts be pleasing to You. Grant me the confidence that whatever I ask in Jesus' name, You will provide. I come before You in faith, acknowledging You as the Alpha and Omega, the source of all existence. As my Creator, You know what is best for me and what will bring glory to Your name. I trust in Your wisdom and seek Your guidance in all things.

In Jesus' name,

Amen

NOTES

"Resilient." Oxford Languages and Google English Dictionary, Oxford University Press, http://www.google.com/resilient. Retrieved 2, Oct. 2022.

"Intentional." Oxford Languages and Google English Dictionary, Oxford University Press, http://www.google.com/intentional. Retrieved 2, Oct. 2022.

"Discipline." Oxford Languages and Google English Dictionary, Oxford University Press, http://www.google.com/discipline. Retrieved 2, Oct. 2022.

"Diligent." Random House Unabridged Dictionary, Random House Inc, http://www.dictionary.com/diligent. Retrieved 2, Apr. 2023.

"Dominion." Oxford Languages and Google English Dictionary, Oxford University Press, http://www.google.com/dominion. Retrieved 2, Oct. 2022.

"Reset." Random House Unabridged Dictionary, Random House Inc, http://www.dictionary.com/reset. Retrieved 2, Oct. 2022

"Obedient." Oxford Languages and Google English Dictionary, Oxford University Press, http://www.google.com/obedient. Retrieved 2, Oct. 2022.

"Freedom." Oxford Languages and Google English Dictionary, Oxford University Press, http://www.google.com/freedom. Retrieved 2, Oct. 2022.

"Reform." Oxford Languages and Google English Dictionary, Oxford University Press, http://www.google.com/reform. Retrieved 2, Oct. 2022.

"Commit." Oxford Languages and Google English Dictionary, Oxford University Press, http://www.google.com/commit. Retrieved 2, Oct. 2022.

"Focus." Random House Unabridged Dictionary, Radom House Inc, http://www.dictionary.com/focus. Retrieved 2, Oct. 2022

"Hope." Oxford Languages and Google English Dictionary, Oxford University Press, http://www.google.com/hope. Retrieved 2, Oct. 2022.

"Believe." Oxford Languages and Google English Dictionary, Oxford University Press, http://www.google.com/believe. Retrieved 2, Oct. 2022.

"Truth." Oxford Languages and Google English Dictionary, Oxford University Press, http://www.google.com/truth. Retrieved 2, Oct. 2022.

"Accountable." Oxford Languages and Google English Dictionary, Oxford University Press, http://www.google.com/accountable. Retrieved 2, Oct. 2022.

"Disingenuous." Oxford Languages and Google English Dictionary, Oxford University Press, http://www.google.com/disingenuous. Retrieved 2, Oct. 2022.

"Justification." Oxford Languages and Google English Dictionary, Oxford University Press, http://www.google.com/justification. Retrieved 2, Oct. 2022.

"Revive." Oxford Languages and Google English Dictionary, Oxford University Press, http://www.google.com/revive. Retrieved 2, Oct. 2022.

"Steadfast." Oxford Languages and Google English Dictionary, Oxford University Press, http://www.google.com/steadfast. Retrieved 2, Oct. 2022.

"Conqueror."Merriam-Webster.com Dictionary, Merriam-Webster, https://www.merriam-webster.com/dictionary/conqueror. Accessed 2, Oct. 2022.

"Authentic." Oxford Languages and Google English Dictionary, Oxford University Press, http://www.google.com/authentic. Retrieved October 2, 2022.

"Adapt." Oxford Languages and Google English Dictionary, Oxford University Press, http://www.google.com/adapt. Retrieved 2, Oct. 2022.

"Inspire." Oxford Languages and Google English Dictionary, Oxford University Press, http://www.google.com/inspire. Retrieved 2, Oct. 2022.

"Prayer." Oxford Languages and Google English Dictionary, Oxford University Press, http://www.google.com/prayer. Retrieved 2, Oct. 2022.

ABOUT THE AUTHOR

Kenya Z. Edwards, also known as Kay, was born and raised in the Borough of Brooklyn, New York. With a penchant for classic black and white movies and an insatiable sweet tooth, her excitement for life is reflected in her eclectic interests and vibrant personality.

As the host of a weekly show, *What Would Kay Say?* on Radio Free Brooklyn, Kay's main goal is to captivate audiences through engaging discussions and insightful commentary. She invites listeners into a world of introspection and inspiration.

Before fully embracing her calling to serve God, Kay navigated a dynamic career path that traversed the realms of finance, telecommunications, and education. However, it wasn't until she found her heart's true passion that her professional trajectory took on deeper meaning. Driven by a profound sense of purpose, Kay redirected her focus towards serving God wholeheartedly. Through her faith-filled journey, she discovered a calling to inspire and uplift others.

Today, Kay's commitment to spiritual service permeates every aspect of her life, infusing her broadcast endeavors with authenticity, compassion, and unwavering faith. Kay channels her passion for community empowerment and social change, further enriching her dedication to making a difference in the world.

Connect with Kay on social media and tune in to *What Would Kay Say?* to embark on a journey of discovery, reflection, and transformation.

www.ingramcontent.com/pod-product-compliance
Lightning Source LLC
Chambersburg PA
CBHW051523120626
46551CB00012B/1052